From Pictures

The story of writing

written by *Jillian Powell* and *Irene Yates*
illustrated by *Mike Fisher*

How did writing begin?	2
The earliest writing	4
Egyptian hieroglyphs	6
Chinese characters	8
Alphabets	10
Writing materials	12
Scribes	14
Calligraphy	16
Printing	18
Writing around the world	20
Word processing	22
Glossary	24

How did writing begin?

People have used words to talk to each other for at least 100 000 years. About 5000 years ago, they began to write words down. Writing is a way of storing and passing on information.

All writing began with pictures. From about 20 000 BC, Stone Age peoples began drawing pictures of animals on cave walls. They signed their pictures by making hand-prints.

The earliest autograph – a hand-print by a Stone Age cave painter

About 3000 BC, the Sumerian people, who lived in the Middle East, began to keep records by drawing pictures on clay tablets. We call these pictures pictographs. They are pictures that have a meaning.

The Aztecs, who lived in Mexico (1300–1500 AD), used pictographs to write about farming, history and religion. They wrote on stone, animal skins and paper made from tree bark.

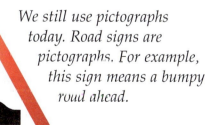

We still use pictographs today. Road signs are pictographs. For example, this sign means a bumpy road ahead.

The earliest writing

The Sumerian people invented hundreds of signs for their writing. They used sharp tools made from reed, bone or metal, and drew on blocks of clay about the size of a postcard. They dried the clay blocks in the sun.
The earliest writings showed how many cows and how many sacks of grain farmers owned.

Over hundreds of years, the signs became simpler. Straight lines were the clearest to read, so simple signs with straight edges were used.

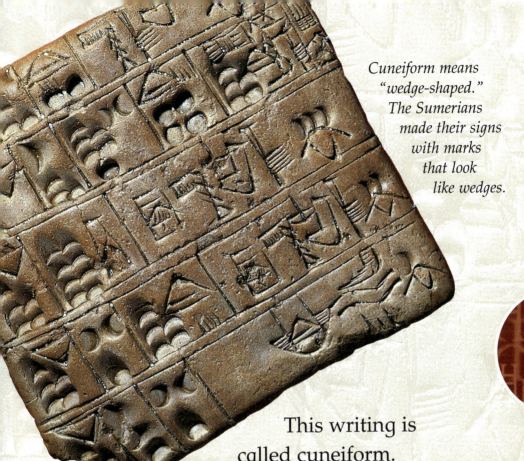

Cuneiform means "wedge-shaped." The Sumerians made their signs with marks that look like wedges.

This writing is called cuneiform.

The signs the Sumerians made could represent words or ideas. A foot sign could mean "foot" or "walking." Later, some of the signs began to stand for sounds as well as words and ideas. The word for fish was "ha." So a fish sign could be used to represent the sound "ha" in another word.

Egyptian hieroglyphs

Around 3000 BC the Ancient Egyptians invented signs called hieroglyphs. Many were pictures of birds, animals or people. But hieroglyphs could be used to describe ideas as well as objects. A crying eye could show sadness. Two wavy lines could mean water or show that something was wet. Later, hieroglyphs that represented sounds were added.

The Rosetta Stone. The top section of writing is in hieroglyphs.

The Ancient Egyptians wrote with pens or brushes made from reeds. They wrote on walls, statues, mummy cases and **papyrus scrolls**.

The word hieroglyph means "sacred writing," because the signs were used in temples and on tombs.

Papyrus is a kind of paper, made from the reeds that grow on the banks of the River Nile.

Hieroglyphs were used for nearly 4000 years. Sometimes they had to be read from left to right, but sometimes they went from right to left or top to bottom.

The Mayan people, who lived in South America, also used a form of writing based on hieroglyphs.

Chinese characters

While the Ancient Egyptians were writing with hieroglyphs, the Chinese were developing another form of writing. They invented thousands of different signs called **characters**. The characters represented objects, ideas or sounds.

The earliest Chinese writing was written by fortune-tellers on animal bones and tortoise-shells. Pottery and silk were also written on. They used brushes made from animal hair dipped in red or black ink.

Around 100 BC, the Chinese began making paper using bamboo, leaves or tree bark.

Chinese writing spread to Japan and other Eastern countries, who then developed their own characters.

There are over 50 000 characters in Chinese writing. Chinese children will probably learn about 4000 of them. Every time something new is invented, a new character must be invented too. A Chinese child will have special classes to teach them the art of **calligraphy**.

Alphabets

An alphabet is a system of letters that represent sounds. They can be joined together to make words. The first alphabet was invented around 1000 BC by the Phoenicians, who lived along the shores of the Mediterranean.

Alphabets made it much easier to write. Instead of learning hundreds of different signs or characters, people could just learn the letters of the alphabet and put them together to make lots of different words. Every word in the English language can be written using just 26 letters.

The Phoenicians were traders. Their way of writing soon spread to other parts of the world.

There are over 60 different alphabets used in the world today. The longest alphabet is Khmer, used in Cambodia, with 74 letters.

The Greeks experimented with ways of writing, including spirals.

The Ancient Greeks borrowed Phoenician letters. They changed some letters and added vowel sounds to make the Greek alphabet. The Romans borrowed some Greek letters. They changed some letters and added to them to make the Roman alphabet. This is the alphabet we use to write English and other western languages today.

The Vikings used an alphabet made from letters called runes. They thought runes had magic powers and used them to write charms and curses.

Writing materials

Before pens were invented, people wrote with sharp bits of bone or reed, or paint brushes made from animal hair. **Quill pens**, made from the feathers of swans or geese, were used from around 500 BC. They were used until the 1800s when they began to be replaced by pens with steel **nibs**.

Queen Elizabeth I wrote with a quill pen.

The Romans wrote on wax tablets.

Until the 1840s, school children in Britain wrote on slates using chalk. The writing could be rubbed out and the slate could be used many times.

Before paper was invented people wrote on stone, bones, clay, tree bark, leaves and silk. The Ancient Egyptians wrote on papyrus, and later used parchment, made from animal skins. The Chinese invented paper made from bamboo and other plants around 100 AD. In Europe, paper did not replace parchment until the 1400s.

Scribes

Before printing was invented, all books had to be copied out by hand. It could take many months or even years to copy a book, so books were very expensive.

The people who copied books were called scribes. Scribes went to writing schools to learn their skill.

In Jewish synagogues, scribes are still employed to copy out the Hebrew scriptures by hand.

In Ancient Egypt, scribes were well paid and respected as much as doctors and priests.

The Ancient Egyptians believed their god Thoth created writing as a gift to the world.

In Europe, if you were a student in **medieval** times, you had to copy the books you needed. Scribes copied books on cookery, medicine and poetry for rich people. Monasteries had their own writing rooms, where monks copied the Bible, prayer books and other religious works.

A Chinese legend says that writing was a gift to an Emperor from a magic tortoise he had saved from drowning.

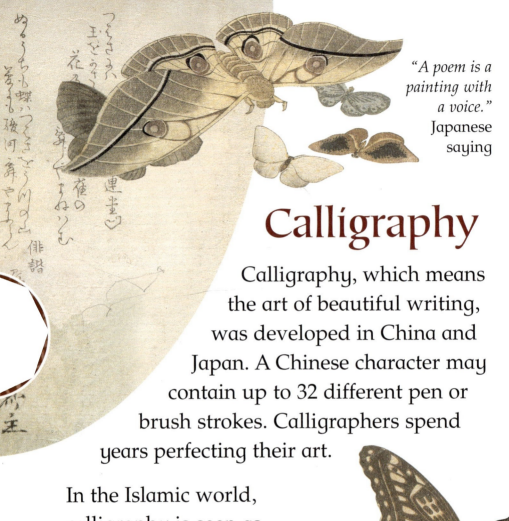

"A poem is a painting with a voice."
Japanese saying

Calligraphy

Calligraphy, which means the art of beautiful writing, was developed in China and Japan. A Chinese character may contain up to 32 different pen or brush strokes. Calligraphers spend years perfecting their art.

In the Islamic world, calligraphy is seen as the greatest art form, because writing is a way of worshipping God. Beautiful Arabic writing decorates holy books, mosques, textiles and pottery.

Many medieval books were beautifully written and decorated. They were made from parchment which was very expensive. It could take the skins of a whole flock of sheep to make just one book. So the monks filled every space on the parchment with letters and pictures. They used bright colours and gold leaf. Books decorated like this are described as **illuminated**.

An illuminated book

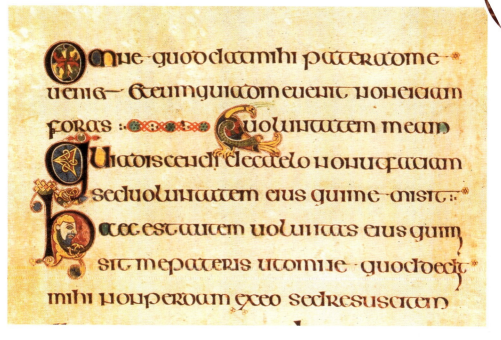

Printing

The Chinese invented printing around 1000 AD. They carved a block of wood for each page of characters. Later, they used pottery characters that could be moved around and used lots of times.

By 1400, Europeans had learned how to print with wooden blocks. The first **printing press** was invented by Johannes Gutenberg in Germany in 1438. He used metal letters that could be moved around.

The earliest known book is the Diamond Sutra, *which was block printed in China in 868 AD.*

This is what the first printing press would have looked like.

A printing press could print as many pages in one day as a scribe could write in one year. Gutenberg's press was worked by hand, but by 1811 printing presses were powered by steam. This made printing even faster. Books became much cheaper and ordinary people could afford to buy them.

Writing around the world

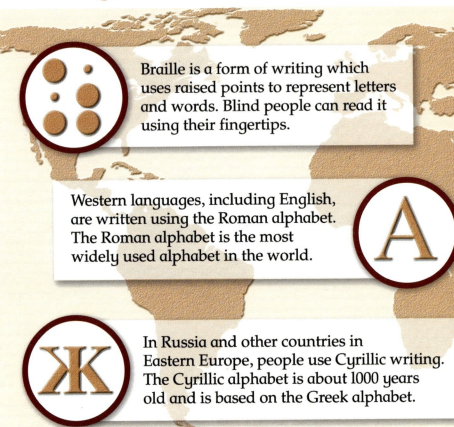

Braille is a form of writing which uses raised points to represent letters and words. Blind people can read it using their fingertips.

Western languages, including English, are written using the Roman alphabet. The Roman alphabet is the most widely used alphabet in the world.

In Russia and other countries in Eastern Europe, people use Cyrillic writing. The Cyrillic alphabet is about 1000 years old and is based on the Greek alphabet.

Today people around the world use many different forms of writing.

 Hebrew is the ancient language of the Bible and is used in Israel today. It is written from right to left, and uses dots and dashes to show vowel sounds.

There are many different forms of writing in India. Some use letters based on the Phoenician alphabet.

 Arabic and Muslim peoples use Arabic writing. It is written from right to left. Vowels are written as signs above and below the letters.

Some, like the Chinese and Japanese, use signs or characters that represent words and ideas. Most use an alphabet with letters that stand for sounds.

Word processing

Typewriters were invented in the 1860s so that people could print out their own writing. By the 1950s, typewriters were powered by electricity which made typing faster and easier.

People began to use computers as word processors in the 1960s. Computers can store writing and print it out in many different ways, using different **fonts** and different sizes. They make it easy for people to write information down and pass it on to other people.

E-mail is short for electronic mail. It is used to send written messages through the Internet. It means that people can write to each other without using pens or paper, or stamps or envelopes. It is fast and easy to send information all around the world.

Writing has come a long way since the days of clay tablets and reed pens! Writing has come a long way since the days of clay tablets and reed pens! Writing has come a long way since the days of clay tablets and reed pens! Writing has come a long way since the days of clay tablets and reed pens! Writing has come a long way since the days of clay tablets and reed pens! Writing has come a long way since the days of clay tablets and reed pens! Writing has come a long way since the days of clay tablets and reed pens! Writing has come a long way since the days of clay tablets and reed pens! Writing has come a long way since the days of clay tablets and reed pens!

Glossary

calligraphy the art of beautiful writing

character any symbol used for writing

font a style of lettering on a computer or typewriter

illuminate to add coloured letters, designs or pictures to a page

medieval from the Middle Ages (about 1000 to 1400 AD)

nib the writing point of a pen

papyrus an early type of paper made from papyrus reeds

printing press a machine that puts words and pictures on to paper

quill pen a pen made from a bird's feather

scroll a roll of paper, parchment or papyrus used to write on

synagogue the Jewish place of worship

typewriter a machine for printing typed words